The Master Relationship Builder

Relationship Building Through the Eyes
of the Employee

LJ Crawford

Limits of Liability and Disclaimer of Warranty

Warning – Disclaimer

THE MASTER RELATIONSHIP BUILDER

Copyright © 2014 by LJ Crawford

ISBN: 978-1-941749-37-1

4-P Publishing

Chattanooga, TN 37411

LJ Crawford
LjtheSpeaker@gmail.com
Ljcmotivations.com

Acknowledgements

I am thankful God is truly the master relationship builder in my life, giving me the ability to transform life's trials and tribulations into actions and victories.

Many people deserve thanks for accompanying me on this journey, my mother, Ms. Gloria Crawford-McDonald, my children, Corey and Jazmyn Moss and my wonderful sisters and brothers. God blessed me with a supportive family who demands me to chase my dreams and aspirations.

Much gratitude to a host of true friends who are always there to laugh, cry, and brainstorm with me.

To the S.W.A.T. Book Camp and The Empowerment Center, to God be the glory of our union.

CONTENTS

INTRODUCTION

I developed The Master Relationship Builder from a special place in my heart for the fair treatment of people. The purpose of this book is simple and twofold. First, to let employees know someone understands the days they go home in utter confusion about mistreatment by a leader. Secondly, to help leaders understand their ability to lead affects culture and employee loyalty. I firmly believe if leaders can truly learn to lead with fairness, integrity, and respect, the workplace will be a place of continuous learning, development, and growth.

1

RELATIONSHIPS

If you want to go fast go alone; if you want to go far go with others

- African Proverb

The word relationship can evoke thoughts of togetherness, love, and loyalty, or a memory of anger, pain, and disrespect.

We don't always talk about workplace relationships – why? Perhaps because their relevance is unclear.

Merriam Webster defines relationship as:

The way in which two or more people, groups, etc. talk to, behave, and deal with each other.

Relationships should be just as important in business as budget and bottom line. Without a positive relationship between managers and their employees, there may be no need for a budget, as there will be no repeat business or stability within the company. Employees want to feel they are part of something bigger than a job.

Is it possible for employers to spend time with each employee on a daily basis and give 100 percent to that interaction? Probably not, and employees don't expect it, but they do need leaders who listen when they speak and engage in genuine conversations with them.

How hard is this for a small company? Not very, as in small company leaders see their employees in passing several times a day. Do leaders take the time to ask how they're doing? How are kids and family, or life outside work? This requires minimal effort, but can make a big difference in employee morale.

Some leaders refuse to take this step, simple as it is. At one point in my life, I lost my home. Though I was living in hotels and bouncing between the homes of generous friends, I never missed work and smiled in spite of my situation.

During that time, a leader discussed a problem with me which seemed so small I felt compelled to share a real life issue. I replied, "Did you know I am currently homeless?"

"Why would I know that?!" he replied.

An employee can give years of service to an organization only to realize their leader knows nothing about them as an individual.

Will every company care about building genuine relationships with employees? No, and to some extent that is okay, because some companies can afford high turnover – if someone moves on because they are unhappy, someone else will always quickly fill that position. But when the business involves customer service and clients, healthy relationships within the company are crucial so clients can work with the same person in the long term. Leaders should realize the lack of internal relationship building not only affects employees but clients as well.

Many resources out there focus on building employee morale, which "should create" employee-employer relationships, but when the team-building activities are over, what keeps that sense of unity moving forward? It's simple but requires a genuine desire to keep the process moving: regularly learn something new about each employee and care. Caring for each other and building intentional workplace relationships leads to a company or department efficiently staffed by people who feel valued, appreciated, and included.

When I shared the concept of this book with others, many of them told me the new world of business doesn't care about building relationships internally. This is because where one employee will not work and be happy, another applicant will gladly step in. But isn't it better to relate to employees and encourage them to continue being part of a vision, instead of always training new employees and working with disgruntled old ones?

Many companies spend thousands on programs teaching about various personality traits and learning styles. All of this is wasted if the techniques are not implemented. Like most of us, I have taken many such assessments. In one workplace, I learned through an assessment my boss was a very analytical person. He hated fluff, just give him the facts and keep it moving. As for myself, I am a dolphin - happy and talkative and full of fun stories. This manager could not and did not want to understand me; it took me an entire year to wrap my mind around this type of personality so different from mine. The adapting did not come from management, but from me. If you love what you do, sometimes the change must begin with you.

The saddest part for me is wanting to build a personable relationship with my manager, but knowing I can't. How many employees feel this way?

Is it necessary to have a personal relationship with workplace leaders to receive a paycheck? Absolutely not, but employees are more motivated when they do and feel more anchored in their position.

Managers, will your direct reports remember their relationship with you as one of respect and admiration? Or as "I would never work at that company again as long as he/she is still in charge?" The choice is yours.

Thoughts

_____

2

TRUST

Trust is a fragile thing: easy to break, easy to lose, and one of the hardest things to ever get back.

- *Zig Ziglar*

Every relationship, whether personal or business, is rooted in trust. How many employees can say trust is the foundation of their work relationships? Employees want to feel leaders support the decisions they make and allow them to do their jobs efficiently. Lack of trust exists for different reasons – some leaders purposely do not support employees   in an effort to eliminate them by proving they are incapable of doing their jobs.

The second job I held tainted my ability to trust in the workplace though I try not to take the past into new job experiences.

In the 90s, I worked for a company where I fulfilled two positions. My supervisor always said I did a great job. I would ask for direction if needed, and thought everything was great. When I received my annual bonus, my manager commented I was not doing my job, and clearly there were problems in my department. Accompanied by no other feedback, did this build my trust in her as my leader? Of course not, and I eventually left the company, predictably, because it's difficult to give your best with no real support or clear expectations.

When I presented my concerns to a general manager, she was flabbergasted as she esteemed me as a hard worker. Unfortunately, her position forced her to support my direct manager. Situations like this are common, but managers are not always right by default of their job title.

In another work environment, I once spent a few weeks questioning one of my checks, but neither of two leaders responded to my requests for a recalculation of the numbers. Finally, I asked one of them to give me the paperwork so I could recalculate on my own. The leaders discussed this, and when I returned to my desk, I had an email stating I was not to recalculate on my work time because their calculations were correct.

I felt infuriated to the point of tears. At this point, my irritation was not about the money, but about such childlike behavior over a simple question. I did as directed and came in to work on a Sunday night to recalculate. Were there mistakes? Yes – though not big enough to make much of a difference. But the fact two members of a leadership team would fight so hard not to help me created an irreparable lack of trust. That was years ago, but I still remember being suspicious of these leaders after that incident. My thoughts were always: Why are you being pleasant? Are you plotting against me as you're smiling at me?

It's sad and demotivating to place no trust or faith in those who make overarching company decisions. If leaders can't be fair even in minor issues, how can you trust them to be diplomatic and unbiased in anything?

Inconsistency also contributes to lack of trust. Consistency means maintaining similar expectations across the board for all employees. Employees often see leaders protect certain favored employees, yet discipline others for the same behavior. Favoritism often combats respect in the workplace – the hardest worker who cares the most is disregarded while slacker coworkers enjoy praise.

Once, a young colleague reported I was "mean" because I had taken an abrupt tone on a few occasions. I was immediately pulled into an office with three directors to discuss my alleged harsh and cruel behavior. I was shocked, as the complaint came from someone who could be quite rude themselves and rarely took time to speak to me.

One of the directors let me know policy required we discuss the complaint against me. When I later broached a concern about a difficult manager, one of the same leaders responded with a curt, "Maybe it's time you look for another job."

A leader who strives to be fair to everyone may not always be popular, but will be respected.

Leaders should create a work environment encouraging personal and professional growth for each employee. Not everyone on the payroll wants to be in management or be a leader. Those who do are hesitant to move up if they don't trust leadership to have their best interests at heart once they advance into a new role.

Leaders, be mindful of your actions towards your employees. You can drag them along with you, or lead with the integrity and fairness they want to follow.

Thoughts

_____

3

COMMUNICATION

The basic building block of good communication

is the feeling that every human being is unique

and of value.

- Unknown

L ack of communication is to blame for the demise of most relationships as it is a crucial part of relationship building. While some leaders would swear on a stack of Bibles they are excellent communicators, their employees may disagree. Emails get the job done, but what about a simple communication method we're born with – vocal cords?

We communicate through two types of communication: verbal and nonverbal, or body language. Consider how children respond to these types of communication – no matter how much they listen, they will eventually do what you do. Leaders play the role of a parent in a sense, and should be mindful of the behavior they model for their employees.

Delivery of verbal communication is vital – it's important to think about how they will perceive the information you discuss with someone. I have reported to leaders who spoke to me in such a condescending way that I could not absorb the information. The words were relevant, but the delivery was so poor I could not firmly grasp the instructions.

You have probably worked with managers whom you would rather email than speak to in person. This is a painful way to work with someone on a daily basis, and many leaders don't recognize this dynamic. Of course not all of them suffer from this inability to communicate. I've taken several informal polls and find it mind-blowing how many employees find speaking with their employer like riding a roller coaster - one day full of laughter and joy and the next day short and irritated.

Leaders, use your words. Often, an employee wants to give his or her best to the company, and it's clear to everyone, yet somehow overlooked by the person whose opinion matters most.

I have been told I would never be successful in business because of my friendly personality and talkative nature. Surely the manager could have chosen another way to tell me to keep folks out of my office during selling time. The funny thing is: when it was mentioned to me, I had already recognized the issue and had begun better regulating who was in and out of my office. But the leader didn't ask me any questions before hammering me with negative words. As a result, I battled self-doubt of my ability to produce the results expected of me.

The tone of voice, is another aspect of verbal communication which proves critical in whether an employee hears instructions or constructive criticism. Though leaders intend to just ask a question about an issue, the tone of voice is often condescending or accusatory. I have experienced this throughout my career in interactions with various supervisors.

That tone causes employees to feel defensive, particularly competent employees who have probably already handled the issue at hand. From the subordinate perspective, it seems as though leaders will typically assume you don't know what you're doing no matter how hard you try to prove your abilities.

On the other hand, I have shared workspace with a manager who did not speak to me for a full week. During that week of silence, I lost trust in my boss. I wondered if I had done something wrong or if it was just my turn to be ignored. No employee should feel so alienated by the one who is supposed to guide them to greatness within their company.

Some leaders even yell at their employees. A job title should not create a superhuman, incapable of understanding that employees are people with feelings who deserve to be treated with respect.

Imagine coming to work with a migraine you have been silently nursing for several days. A manager calls you to ask a question but commences yelling when you don't immediately know the answer. When I found myself in this situation, I simply hung up.

As I left my office to find the answer to this urgent question, suddenly the same manager is screaming in my face about this question which could be easily answered in five minutes of calm.

He then shook his finger in my face, chastising me in the middle of the open hallway, and threatened to complain to human resources for my disrespect in hanging up on him.

After many months, I finally received an apology, but so much of my respect for this person had died. If verbal communication had been different in this scenario, a respectful relationship would still be alive.

Leaders often overlook the importance of body language unless they are analyzing a new employee though employees analyze their leaders on a daily basis.

Eye contact is one of my top two irritants when it comes to body language. In an intimate meeting, if a leader establishes eye contact with everyone in the room but one employee, that person will notice.

Another aspect of body language in the workplace is what I call the square-off − when a leader joins a group of employees, they tend to stand with shoulders squared toward those included in the conversation. The new circle often excludes someone, making them feel as if they are not part of the team or part of the leader's vision for the team. Employee performance decreases as a result. Though silent, body language screams the true thoughts of the leader.

Thoughts

_____

4

TOXIC ENVIRONMENTS

If someone shows you who they are, believe them.

\- *Maya Angelou*

This is an emotional chapter for me – when you love your job, but you're taking antidepressants just to be able to drive up to the building –that is a problem.

I have been in the workforce since I was 17 and over time I have experienced both discrimination and disappointment in leadership whose words and actions have hurt me to my core. I've struggled with feeling of unworthiness. I've been ignored as if I were not a part of the team or even in the room during meetings. I've stood outside of the favoritism circle. Through it all I have kept my faith and kept moving.

We all need to make a living, and if we must work for someone else, we want to work in a positive, upbeat environment. This is not a fairytale – I have worked in one environment that was so healthy and encouraging that I wanted to come in early and stay late. It's wonderful to enter your workplace and feel at home.

The responsibility of detoxifying a toxic environment begins with leadership though employees have to trust the plan and be willing to start fresh.

I've heard long speeches from leaders on how managers should speak to everyone and give praise for hard work. I've come away from such talks excited to embark on a new way of life at the company, only to be disappointed the very next day.

I tend to give the benefit of the doubt whenever possible, but recall one leader with a unique personality. When I first met her, I attempted friendly conversation but found her standoffish. Yet when she interacted with certain others, she spoke with infectious volume and laughter. I soon learned she just didn't care for me and it was okay if I didn't always make small talk.

Toxic work environments have caused me stress levels so high I've passed out at work and been rushed to the hospital and immediately put on a morphine pump. I've been on two antidepressants, I have an ulcer, sleep has eluded me, and depression has nearly destroyed me. Even in those situations, I've loved what I do, and clients have let me know they would not patronize that business if not for me.

I am thankful for those who have helped me along the way so I can now help others detoxify and be positive until a change occurs.

Thoughts

5

RESPECT

*If you have some respect for people as they are,
you can be more effective in helping them to
become better than they are.*

-   John W. Gardner

First, relationship building requires mutual respect. Employees sincerely need to respect and look up to their leader or supervisor. It makes sense if someone is going to provide leadership to a team, they should possess qualities employees might want to emulate. Employees feel total disdain toward leaders who treat them disrespectfully.

It's easy for a leader to get rid of an employee who doesn't show respect for them or to clients, but what can an employee do about a disrespectful manager? Either find other employment or go home miserable every day for the sake of a paycheck. Some people have an internal drive strong enough to ignore negative behavior. They can respect a position even if they don't respect the person in it. Though difficult, it is sometimes necessary for those who love what they do.

I have seen managers yell at employees with such disrespect it literally made me sick to my stomach, but more sickening was the upper management who made excuses for these managers. Where is the integrity to speak to another person with the same respect they are expected to give you? When employees who have been mistreated are promoted, yelling, screaming, and poisoned behavior continues. This is not conducive to a great product, to great customer service, or to a supportive learning environment. Your job becomes just a place to get a paycheck.

In one job I've held, I ended up in a management position after several promotions. When the company became short staffed, leadership wanted me to fulfill the duties of the very first position I had held there in addition to my actual position at that time. Because I was the only one asked to do this, I believe the request grew out of disrespect for me. Even if they didn't think of it that way, perception is everything.

As children, we're taught to treat others as we want to be treated. Judging by the way some leaders treat their employees, many of us forget this important lesson. Leaders, ask yourself if you would want your daughter, son, wife or parent to have you for a boss? If you can honestly answer yes, keep up the good work, but if you hesitate, reevaluate yourself and your behavior.

Thoughts

_____

6

THE MASTER RELATIONSHIP BUILDER

How far you go in life depends on your being tender with the young, compassionate with the aged, sympathetic with the striving, and tolerant of the weak and strong – because someday in your life you will have been all of these.

- *George Washington Carver*

Becoming a master relationship builder requires an internal drive, need, and determination. You must reach within to recognize areas which need improvement, take responsibility for them, and strive daily to be better. CEOs, directors, managers, and supervisors, you are captains. Notice your behavior as you guide your employees. They look to you for direction and help, but you cannot effectively support them if you have lost their trust and respect.

I hope this book helps leaders become aware of their behavior toward their employees and future leaders. Praise those who love what they do and are faithful to your company. You would be surprised at the level of productivity you can achieve through praise. I can recall one-on-ones with my managers focused so heavily on the negative though I knew I gave my best and wanted to learn. The feedback I received deflated my spirit so much I wanted to quit. But others' opinions do not define me. Had I allowed negative words to push me down, I would not have the knowledge that I do now.

No relationship building took place under many managers I have worked with, and I constantly battled to gain any kind of trust or respect from them. But they helped me learn some hard lessons about dealing with various individuals, and I am now a master of recognizing management styles.

I have also been blessed to experience a manager whom I would not let in because she appeared to be most of the negative things we've discussed in this book. But eventually we talked about how I was feeling under her management. She listened, understood my learning style, and began to build trust with me. When all was said and done, I would do anything for her. She truly embodied the qualities of a master relationship builder.

If you are a manager who genuinely cares about employees, you should remember the relevance of:

• **Relationship building** - Relationships are crucial to effectiveness.

• **Trust** - It's the foundation of healthy relationships.

• **Communication-** Communicate with staff, letting them know they are valued and part of the company vision. Take the time to speak so employees know they are more than warm bodies filling positions.

• **Environment** - If you misbehave without any accountability, employees mimic your behavior, creating a pool of toxicity.

• **Respect** - Treat others as you want to be treated.

A master relationship builder creates a phenomenal team with little turnover, and everyone understands the vision of the team and the company. Leaders, be a master at building individuals. Be a master at taking them to the next level of personal and professional growth. You will not only be amazed at their growth and your team's effectiveness, but you will also have the internal satisfaction of knowing you have helped someone else.

Teamwork is the ability to work together toward a common vision. It is the ability to direct individual accomplishments towards organizational objectives. It is the fuel that allows common people to attain uncommon results.

- Andrew Carnegie

Thoughts

ABOUT THE AUTHOR

Lisa J. Crawford is the founder of LJC Motivations where she focuses on training and motivating others to reach their highest potential. She is a Certified Purpose Discovery Specialist and a Certified City Strategist.

Though life has been an uphill journey, LJ has garnered grace, mercy, and lessons of growth along the way.

LJ considers herself a servant to the suffering, and her genuine love for others allows her to counsel and actively guide people to another level of life.

A native of Chattanooga, Tennessee, LJ enjoys spending time with her two wonderful children and two awesome grandchildren.

For speaking engagements, contact LJ at the **themasterrelationshipbuilder@gmail.com**

http://ljcrawford.wix.com/ljcmotivations.